Although the cartoons of Ali Farzat above all address local issues, their visual vocabulary makes them universally appealing and relevant. Farzat utilizes all that he has to hand and takes it as far as possible to create a space for social comment and debate. His pointed caricatures, published in the domestic and foreign press, inspire his readers to reach sincere interpretations of their daily lives and to consider politics, economics, and society from new angles.

—Prince Claus Award Committee
Holland

و رغم أن رسوم فرزات هذه تتناول قضايا محلية في مجملها ، فإن مفرداتها البصرية ترتفع بها إلى مستوى العالمية معنى و قبولا . و فرزات يفيد من كل المعطيات المحيطة به فيستثمرها إلى أبعد الحدود موفرا عبرها ساحة عامة للتعليق و النقاش . إن رسوماته المميزة المنشورة في الصحافة المحلية و العالمية تساعد القراء على الوصول إلى فهم حقيقي لحياتهم اليومية و إلى اعتبار السياسة والاقتصاد و المجتمع من زاويا جديدة .

– لجنة جائزة الأمير كلاوس
هولندا

A Pen of

Damascus Steel

The Political Cartoons of an Arab Master

By Ali Farzat

Cune

A Pen of Damascus Steel: The Political Cartoons of an Arab Master
© 2005 Ali Farzat
Cune Press, Seattle 2005
First Edition
3 5 7 9 8 6 4 2
ISBN (cloth) 978-1885942388   ISBN (paper) 978-1885942395
Calligraphy by Mamoun Sakkal. Production assistance by George Meassy.
Cune Press, PO Box 31024, Seattle, WA 98103 www.cunebooks.com.

Library of Congress Cataloging-in-Publication Data
Farzat, Ali, 1951-
A pen of Damascus steel / by Ali Farzat.
p. cm.
Includes index.
ISBN 978-1-885942-38-8 (cloth) -- ISBN 978-1-885942-39-5(paper)
1. Syria--Politics and government--1971---Caricatures and cartoons.
2. Caricatures and cartoons--Syria. I. Title.
DS98.4.F37 2003
956.9104'2'0222--dc21
2002041149

Other titles in the Bridge between the Cultures Series:

The Road from Damascus: A Journey Through Syria - by Scott C. Davis

Steel & Silk: Men and Women Who Shaped Syria 1900-2000 - by Sami Moubayed

Searching Jenin: Eyewitness Accounts of the Israeli Invasion 2002 - by Ramzy Baroud

For greeting cards and other products featuring cartoons by Ali Farzat visit www.cunepress.com

Content

الظلم

بقلم علي فرزات

هذه المجموعة من الرسوم المنشورة في هذا الكتاب ليست كل ما رسمت . . . فلدي ما يقارب الخمسة عشر ألفاً أخرى من الرسومات الكاريكاتيرية التي تم إعدادها خلال خمسة وثلاثين عاما ، مستمداً أفكاري من واقع تحتار فيه بين الضحك والأسى .

ولذلك فقد خرجت رسوماتي على هذا النحو . . . ربما كانت العناوين الإنسانية التي سعيت إليها من خلال رسوماتي من أجل الحرية . . . والديمقراطية . . . والحب . . . والسلام بين البشرية . . . ضد الأنظمة القمعية . . . والظلم . . . والدكتاتوريات . . . والإرهاب . . . وتدمير البيئة . . . والفساد . . . وما إلى ذلك من ممارسات لا إنسانية . . . بالإضافة إلى خلو رسوماتي من التعليق لتكون الفكرة فقط هي أساس اللغة بين الجميع . . . ربما كل ذلك ساعد على خروج أعمالي من داخل حدود مكاني وزماني لتنطبق على كل مكان وزمان من هذا العالم .

وعلى سبيل المثال . . . عندما عرضت رسوماتي على جمهوري وبلدي وفي العديد من عواصم العالم . . . كانت آراء الزائرين تبدي حماساً وانفعالاً واحداً بالرغم من اختلاف موقعهم الجغرافي . . . والبعض كان يظن بأنني كنت أرسم حال واقعهم في البلد الذي أعرض فيه .

على الجانب الآخر لم يخل الطريق الذي سلكته من متاعب شاقة . . وستولى بعض صفحات الكتاب شرح جزء من هذه المتاعب التي

اعتبرها بالرغم من كل شيء ممتعة وليست سيّئة بالنسبة لي لأنها عرفتني أكثر على جمهور عظيم وقف إلى جانبي في الأوقات العصيبة .

الإنسانية

بقلم سكوت س . ديفيس

تقدم رسوم علي فرزات الكاريكاتيرية السياسية للعالم الناطق باللغة الإنكليزية في هذا الوقت لأن أعماله تعبر عن الخواص الدقيقة اللازمة لإنقاذ الإنسانية من المأزق الذي تتخبط فيه حالياً .

في هذه الأيام ، تجد المتطرفين مسيطرين على جهتي الخط الفاصل بين الشرق والغرب . القادة المتشددون ينالون تأييد الأمد بالهجوم العسكري والهجوم المضاد . ويكسبون الانتخابات باللعب في مخاوف الناس وأما الثقة بهم فينحتوها نحتاً في طيبة الرجال والنساء الذين يعيشون في بلاد أجنبية . ويبدو أن القادة والمواطنين العاديين مقتنعون على حد سواء بأن العالم مليء بالأعداء الذين يتآمرون لأذى ، فنحن نترجم أعمال الأجانب الخيرة على أنها تهديدات . وقعنا في الدوامة حيث يفضي بنا قتل الأبرياء إلى الثأر العسكري الذي يقتل المزيد من الأبرياء ثم تعيد الأحداث نفسها كما في دائرة مفرغة . وكلما تعمقت الدوامة ازداد الحقد والانتقام اتساعاً . ومع أن كافة الفرقاء خاسرون فإن الدوامة تشتد أكثر فأكثر في دورانها وتتسارع خطى القتل والعنف . على أن القوة العسكرية والهجمات الانتحارية والاغتيالات والإجراءات الخشنة لا تؤدي إلى السلام إطلاقاً .

8

Preface

Injustice

By Ali Farzat

The cartoons published in this volume are just a few of the 15,000 that I have created in the last 35 years. Caricatures by definition refer to a surface actuality. Yet the mental space where I conceived and shaped my drawings is more obscure. It is a sub-surface realm that is perplexed, that exists in suspension between joy and grief, laughter and tears.

My drawings reflect their origins. I devoted my cartoons to contemporary ideals: Freedom, Democracy, Love, and Peace. I pitted them against contemporary evils: Injustice, Repression, Dictatorship, Terrorism, Environmental Degradation, Corruption. Yet my drawings also reflect the sub-surface work space where they took shape. They have come to embody the simple and yet complex ambiguity of their creation.

For the most part my caricatures have no labels or captions. Yet they seem to speak to people far removed from the day-to-day circumstances that served as the pretext when they were drawn. I have exhibited my caricatures to the public in several world capitals. After seeing my drawings, viewers often conclude that my drawings were created to comment on specific national events in their own countries.

The road that I have walked has been full of opposition, threats, and trouble. Still, as this book will make plain, hardship has had benefits. My troubles have brought me into contact with sympathetic people, on several continents, who have offered encouragement and support in dark times.

Humanity

By Scott C. Davis

We are presenting the political cartoons of Ali Farzat to the English-speaking world at this time because his work expresses the precise qualities that are needed to rescue humanity from its current predicament.

Following the onset of the Al-Aqsa Intifada in September 2000 and the attacks on the World Trade Center and the Pentagon a year later, extremists on both sides of the East-West divide have been ascendant. Hardliners have captured short term support with military attack and counter attack. They have played on the fears of the people and eroded their trust in the goodness of men and women who live on the other side. Leaders and ordinary citizens alike have seemed convinced that the world is filled with enemies who intend to do harm. People on both sides have interpreted the benign actions of foreigners as threats. Humanity has been caught in a downward spiral where the killing of innocents has led to military reprisal that has killed more innocents,

9

تتوق الغالبية العظمى من الناس في العالم العربي والإسلامي كما في العالم الغربي إلى السلام. الكل يريدون أن ينهوا دراستهم ويحصلون على أعمال جيدة يقومون بها كل يوم. الكل يريدون أن يتزوجوا ويؤسسوا عائلات. يريدون أن يرسلوا أولادهم إلى المدارس لتحصيل العلم وأن يكون لديهم بيوت يسكنونها. إنهم يريدون فرص الحياة والحياة الفعالة كما إنهم يريدون مرونة وطمأنينة المؤسسة العائلية على المدى الطويل مع الأصدقاء والمحيط عموما. يريدون أن يتبادلوا الاحترام مع من يعرفون، يريدون أن تحترم منطقتهم وأمتهم ويريدون العناية بوالديهم والمستقبل الرغيد لأولادهم، كما يريدون حماية أنفسهم وعائلاتهم من أخطار الإجرام والعنف والحروب.

فهل يمكن للناس العاديين في العالم، الوسط الواعي، أن يقهروا المتشددين والمتطرفين؟ ماذا لو حلت حركة صاعدة، وفكر وعمل ناهض مكان القوى السلبية المتجمعة والخوف المتكاثف. يقول اللاهوتيون "إن ما ينهض يقارب". فبالتقارب والاتفاق والانسجام يمكننا البدء بمعالجة المشاكل العويصة التي تعترضنا. نحتاج إلى أن نكفل الحياة على ظهر هذا الكوكب الهش بموارده المائية المحدودة، وجوه الرقيق، ومصادر معادنه المقصورة. نحتاج إلى أن نبتكر مفاهيم الاقتصاد الذي يعين المصادر بدقة وكفاية وفعالية ويضع الاستثمار والعمل على أفضل صعد الاستخدام. ويتوجب على هذه المفاهيم أن تتشارك في ثمار الاستثمار الإنساني وأن تعمل بطريقة عادلة منصفة.

هذا ويمكن أن توقف وتعكس الدوامة. والمطلوب هو جوقة أصوات من الوسط. ونحن نقدم صوت علي فرزات معروضا في هذا المجلد كطريقة لإحداث انهمار الأصوات المعتدلة المطلوبة.

لأكثر من ثلاثين عاما كان علي فرزات وما زال واقفاً ضد العنف والترهيب ومناصراً للحياة الهادئة المسالمة للناس العاديين. موضع سخريته هو الجنرال المزيف الذي يقود جنده إلى المعركة لمجرد أن يقف متفرجا وهم

يذبحون. وموضع السخرية الآخر هم النخبة الثرية التي يبدو أنها تعلو في حصاد الثروة التي زرعها العاملون المجدون بعرق الجبين. كما ترى علي فرزات أيضا يرمي بسهامه البيروقراطيين الذين يميتون الاقتصاد بخمولهم، والشرطة السرية الذين يضرون بالبريء ويجنون عليه بشكوكهم. كما إنه ينتقد عقلية الجماهير التي تسير كالقطيع ويدين افتتانها بالاهتمامات الضحلة والسخيفة. وينتقد فرزات بقوة ممارسات التعذيب في السجون والمعتقلات. هذا وتعطي رسوم فرزات الكاريكاتيرية تعبيرات تفصيلية في التنبيه على المشكلات العامة: تضخم السكان، الفقر، التشرد، الحرب، والاحتلال البيئي.

إن الكاريكاتير السياسي لا يمكنه إلقاء القبض على المجرم وسوقه إلى المحاكمة. ولا يمكنه أن يمنع سياسة الاشتباك العسكري. كما لا يمكنه أن يزيح الطاغية النزوي الغاشم عن السلطة. لكن مضمون رسوم الكاريكاتير التي يضعها فنان أصيل صادق يمكن أن يهمنا نحن الذين في الوسط إلى أن نضم أصواتنا إلى الكورس حتى تصبح سلطة الغالبية العظمى أمرا واقعا ويحترم القادة في الحكومة ودنيا الأعمال طلبات هذه الغالبية. وأخيرا فإن الإنسان العادي في العالم، رجلا وامرأة، هو الذي يضفي السلطة على النظم الاقتصادية والأعمال العالمية والحكومات الوطنية والهيئات الوطنية العملاقة التي يبدو أنها تتحكم بالحياة وتمسك بزمام أمورها. ولا يحتاج الإنسان العادي رجلا وامرأة، إلا إلى أن يوافق لبرهة وأثنين على نبل العمل الإنساني وقدسية الحياة الإنسانية. ومن ثم نستطيع أن نتقدم معا بانسجام إلى شفاء محننا وإتمام نقصنا ولإحداث عالم متين وصحيح وصالح لأولادنا. وإنه لمن الملائم ونحن ننفذ السير أن تحمل راياتنا صورا أبدعها على فرزات.

and then the cycle has repeated itself. As the spiral has deepened, the pool of hatred and revenge has grown broader. Even though all parties have been losers, the spiral has turned more and more rapidly, the pace of killing and violence have quickened. Yet precision bombs, suicide attack, assassination, beheading, and other harsh measures will never bring peace.

In the Arab and Islamic world, as well as in the West, the vast majority of people yearn for peace. Is it possible for the ordinary people of the world, the sensible middle, to defeat extremists and hardliners?

What if the gathering negative forces and the thickening fear were replaced by an upward movement, a rising of thought and action. The theologian Teilhard de Chardin tells us, "All things that rise, converge." In convergence and unity we could begin to tackle the broader problems that face us. We need to ensure life on this fragile planet with its limited supply of water, delicate atmosphere, and finite mineral resources. We need to invent notions of economy that allocate resources precisely and efficiently and make the best use of investment and labor. Yet these notions also must share the fruits of human investment and work in an equitable way.

The downward spiral can be stopped and reversed. Amidst the gloom, elections in Palestine give hope, yet experts predict an even more savage cycle of violence if new leaders are unable to deliver full peace on an impossible time table. In Iraq, elections promise to initiate civil war. What's required is more than an election, or a new leader or a new government or a new negotiating strategy. Ultimately, ordinary people create the landscape in which their leaders move. What's needed is a chorus of voices from the middle to condemn short-sighted policies, to applaud altruism and good judgement wherever they may be found, and to establish themselves as a public conscience that can't be ignored.

We offer the images of Ali Farzat, displayed in this volume, as a way of triggering the avalanche of moderate voices that will be required.

For thirty-five years, Ali Farzat has stood against violence, intimidation, and force to champion the peaceful lives of ordinary men and women. He caricatures the hypocritical general who leads his troops into battle only to stand aside while they are slaughtered. Another target is the wealthy elite who seem to exalt in harvesting the wealth that diligent workers have assiduously cultivated. Farzat also skewers the bureaucrat whose inactivity dooms the economy, and the secret police whose suspicions victimize ordinary folk. He also chastises the herd mentality of the masses and their infatuation with shallow and debased preoccupations. Farzat slashes hard at the problem of torture in jail and prison. Other Farzat caricatures give particularized expression to pressing generic problems: overpopulation, poverty, homelessness, war, and environmental degradation.

A political caricature can't catch a criminal and bring him to trial. It can't veto a policy of military engagement or suicide attack. Nor can it remove a capricious and brutal tyrant from power. But a body of political caricatures by a sincere artist can inspire those of us in the middle to add our voices to the chorus until the power of the vast majority becomes tangible and demands respect from leaders in government and business. Ultimately, it is the citizens of the world who lend power to the economic systems,

كوميديا
بروك أندرسون

يمارس علي فرزات عمله برشاقة في غرفة أخبار ليس فيها لافتات ظاهرة للمؤسسة أو للفعالية . يستقبل الضيوف في غرفته ويجيب على الهاتف بيده اليسرى بينما يستخدم قلما بيده اليمنى ليلامس رسما أمامه – وهو ينظر طيلة الوقت إلى ضيوفه على نحو مطمئن بعينيه الزرقاوين وابتسامته العذبة وكأنه يقول : "لحظة وأكون معكم ."

إن حجم مكتب فرزات الإخباري هو بحجم مستودع مريح ويقع في زقاق في وسط دمشق بعد شارع الباكستان . ومن مركز قيادته هذا يدير فرزات عجلة الصحيفة كل أسبوع ، رسوم كاريكاتورية ومقالات تهزأ بالبيروقراطية والبوليس السري والعسكر والفساد والهدر وسوء الأداء .

إن علي فرزات هو الرسام الكاريكاتوري الأكثر نجاحا في الشرق الأوسط وموضوعه هو الإنسانية . إنه ينظر إلى ما وراء الأخبار . ليس الأحداث بل القوة المحركة خلف الأحداث . ونادرا ما استخدم فرزات الكلمات ولا يرسم صورا تشير إلى أناس أو أماكن بالذات ، لكنه يحافظ على اهتمام المشاهدين بخطوط رسوماته الذكية ويبقى عمله كونيا . ومع أنه تلقى تهديدات بالقتل فإنه لم يتعرض لأي محاولة اغتيال (على عكس صديقه الرسام الفلسطيني ناجي العلي الذي اغتيل في لندن عام 1987) . لقد مارس إنتاج الفن بأعلى مستوياته لسنين عديدة . إن عمله مميز وتتخذه الأجيال الصاعدة مثالا لها في الكاريكاتير العربي . والأكثر أهمية ربما كمثل للفنانين الصغار هو جهود علي فرزات الرائدة لخلق فن وإعلان رسالته بينما يعيش في دولة أمنية ويتجادل مع مراقبة المطبوعات .

بدأ علي فرزات الرسم في الخامسة من عمره ، وكان يحلم بأن يصير رساما كاريكاتوريا محترفا . ومما يذكر من طفولته : أن والده استخدم رجالا لإعادة طلاء منزلهم العائلي . وقبل طلي الوجه الأخير رسم هؤلاء الرجال صورا على الجدار – لمجرد التسلية . وبعد ذلك قاموا بطلاء الوجه

الأخير فوق عملهم الفني وذلك باللون الرئيسي المتفق عليه . وكان علي الصغير قد عمل رسوما تخطيطية لصورهم تلك واحتفظ بها في دفتره . وهكذا تلقى درسا مبكرا في ملاءمة الفن لحاجات العالم .

كان والد علي فرزات يعمل مديرا في دائرة حكومية للإسكان وكان العمل يتطلب مراجعة أكداس من العمل الورقي وتوقيع وختم المستندات ومن ثم أرشفتها . كان أبا لطيفا ومتسامحا ، لم يسبق أن عاقب عليا على قيامه بالرسم على ظهر تلك المستندات الرسمية ، ولربما رأى رأيا في رسومات الغلام راحة له من عمله المهم بل الممل .

في المدرسة الابتدائية كان علي يرسم صورا كاريكاتيرية للمعلمين وعندما اكتشف معلمه ذلك طرده من المدرسة . ولم يسمح له بالعودة إلى المدرسة إلا بعد أن وقف أمام المعلمين والإداريين بحضور والده وقال : "لن أعود إلى رسم صور كاريكاتيرية للمعلمين ." كان علي غلاما مستقيما وصادقا لكن معلميه كانوا صارمين وسخيفين ، الأمر الذي لم يستطع علي أن ينسى اتخاذهم هدفا له . فكان والد علي أن يعود مرات عديدة إلى المدرسة ليستمع إلى تعهد ابنه بأن يسلك السلوك الحسن .

في الثانية عشرة من عمره (وكان في الصف السادس الابتدائي) ، قام علي بنشر أول رسم كاريكاتيري له في جريدة الأيام الدمشقية وجاء رسمه هذا على الصفحة الأولى تحت عنوان يتناول الحرب الجزائرية من أجل الاستقلال وقد أرسل الرسم من دير الزور حيث كان يقيم . بعد ذلك تلقى

the global businesses, the national governments, and the super-national organizations that seem to control life. Ordinary men and women need only agree for a moment or two on the nobility of the human enterprise and the sacredness of human life. Then we can move forward, in unity, to heal our sorrow and loss and to create a solid and true world for our children. As we march, it would be fitting if our banners displayed images by Ali Farzat.

Comedy

By Brooke Anderson

Ali Farzat gracefully goes about his job in a newsroom that has no obvious signs of organization or efficiency. He greets guests in his office, answers a phone call with his left hand while using a pen in his right hand to touch up a drawing—all the while looking at his guests reassuringly with wide blue eyes and a sweet smile, as if to say, "I'll be with you in a moment."

Farzat's news office is the size of a convenience store. It's located in an alley in central Damascus off Pakistan Street. From this headquarters, Farzat manages to spin out a newspaper every week with caricatures and articles that routinely mock bureaucracy, secret police, soldiers, corruption, waste, and inefficiency.*

Ali Farzat is the most successful cartoonist in the Middle East. His subject is humanity. His beat is off the news, not events but the dynamics behind events. Farzat rarely uses words, and never draws pictures indicating specific people or places. Farzat holds the viewer's interest with clever lines and depictions, yet his work is also universal. Although he has received death threats, he has never suffered an assassination attempt (unlike his friend, the Palestinian cartoonist

Naji al-Ali who was shot to death in London in 1987). He has been producing art at a high level for many years. His work is distinctive and is used as a model by the younger generation of Arab caricaturists. What is perhaps more important as an example to young artists is Ali Farzat's pioneering effort to create art, to get his message out, while living in a security state and contending with censorship.

Ali Farzat began drawing at the age of five. As a child in Hama he dreamed of becoming a professional cartoonist. One childhood memory: his father hired men to repaint their family home. Before applying the final coat of paint, these men drew pictures on the wall—simply for their own amusement. Later they painted over their artistic expression with the uniform color that their commercial contract required. Young Ali made sketches of their pictures and preserved them in his sketch pads. At the same time he absorbed a lesson in fitting art to the necessities of the world.

Farzat's father was a director of the state office of housing and registration who processed stacks of paperwork, signing and stamping documents, then filing them. A mild an indulgent man, he never punished young Ali for drawing on the reverse side of these official documents. Perhaps he saw the child's drawings as welcome relief to his important yet tedious work.

In primary school, Farzat drew caricatures of teachers. When his teachers discovered these drawings, they kicked him out of school. He could only return after standing in front of teachers, administrators, and his father and saying, "I will never again draw caricatures of teachers." Ali was an honest and sincere child, but his teachers were both strict and foolish,

*Farzat's newspaper was shut down in July 2003.

كتابا من صاحب الجريدة يدعوه فيه إلى دمشق ليقدم رسوما كاريكاتيرية للنشر . ويتذكر علي فرزات ذلك بقوله "لم يكن يعلم أنني في الثانية عشرة من العمر فخاطبني في رسالته بصيغة الجمع الرسمية" .

في عام 1969 وهو في الثامنة عشرة من عمره انتقل علي فرزات إلى دمشق ليفتش عن عمل كرسام كاريكاتيري . وكانت الصحف المستقلة السورية قد أغلقت عام 1963 عندما استلم حزب البعث السلطة . كانت العائدات هزيلة . فعاش على ضآلة المدخرات وسكن في غرفة صغيرة مع صديق جاء دراسة له من حماة . ولم تكن الغرفة تتسع لأكثر من سرير فكان ينام عليه بالتناوب مع صديقه الذي كان يعمل نهارا وينام ليلا بينما كان علي ينام ليلا وينام نهارا . وهذه هي أصل عادة العمل الليلي لعلي فرزات . كان صديقه يعجب ويعلق على رسوماته . وفي آخر الأمر ابتدأ الحصول على قبول للاشتراك بالمعارض . وبعد ستة أشهر من هذه الحُمية استقر فرزات على عمل في جريدة الثورة .

من ذلك الحين برزت رسومات علي فرزات في 28 من المعارض الخاصة أو الجماعية . بدءاً من عام 1990 ولمدة عشر سنوات وستة أيام في الأسبوع ظهرت رسوماته على صفحة الافتتاحية لجريدة تشرين وهي كبرى الصحف الحكومية . وأقتبس من SYRIA-ONLINE.COM .

الماضية شعيرة يومية للحياة الثقافية السورية : كانت صيحات غاضبة في قالب من الفكاهة لتعبر عن كل الإحباطات وخيبات الأمل الشخصية والوطنية والعربية لمشكلات العصر الحاضر" .

الحكمة
بسام طالب

التقيت بعلي فرزات أول مرة عام 1970 في أثناء تأدينا للخدمة العسكرية الإلزامية ، حيث جمعنا مكان واحد وهو العمل في مجلة الشعب . جاء علي ليعمل كفنان ورسام للمجلة وكنت قد سبقته للعمل كسكرتير تحرير للمجلة .

بداية علاقتنا كانت إثر دفاعي عن رسم كاريكاتيري رسمه علي ليكون غلافاً للمجلة وقد رفض المشرف على المجلة آنذاك قبول هذا الرسم بحجة أن المجلة رصينة وجادة ، فطلبت إعفائي من العمل إذا لم تنشر اللوحة التي رسمها علي ، وقد سوّي الأمر ونشرت اللوحة .

لقد خُلق علي ليرسم فموهبته وحضوره وريشته الساحرة غير مرتبطة بتاريخ أو تأهيل ، أو زمان ومكان ، فهو يرسم في أي وقت وفي أي مكان كان ، في الشارع ، في السيارة ، في البيت وفي المطعم .

في يوم من أوائل عام 1970 كنا نستمع إلى محاضرة لضابط ذو رتبة عالية ويتقلد أوسمة كثيرة وكان يحدثنا عن تجربته المريرة وبطولاته وما تجشمه من عناء ومصاعب حتى أصبح قائدا عسكريا ناجحا . ولكم أن تتصوروا كم كان حديثه مملا وكلامه مكررا ومعادا . نظرت إلى علي وكان بجانبي وإذ به يتناول منديلا ورقيا وبدأ يرسم عليه صورتين منفصلتين للمحاضر ، إحدى الصورتين تمثل المحاضر مرتديا بزته الرسمية متقلدا كافة أوسمته نافخا صدره إلى الأعلى ويتكلم بعزة وعنفوان إلى جمهور خامل ومجامل والصورة الثانية تمثل المحاضر في منزله وهو يقف بثيابه الداخلية مرخيا كتفيه حانيا رأسه وهو يستمع إلى تأنيب زوجته وصراخها في وجهه .

targets that he simply could not ignore. His father made many trips to school to hear his son's promise of good behavior.

At age 12 (when he was in the sixth grade) Farzat published his first drawing in a Damascus-based newspaper, *Al-Ayyam (The Days)*. His art ran on the front page under a headline about the Algerian war of independence. He had submitted his drawing from his home in Hama. Later, the owner of the newspaper wrote Farzat a letter, asking him to come to Damascus to draw caricatures for the publication. "He had no idea I was only twelve years old—a sixth grader," recalls Farzat. "In the letter, he addressed me in the formal second person plural!"

In 1969 at age 18, Ali Farzat moved to Damascus to look for work as a caricaturist. Syria's independent newspapers had been closed down in 1963 when the Baath Party took power. (For that matter, Farzat's first published cartoon appeared in the newspaper *Al-Ayyam (The Days)* in 1963, apparently during the last weeks of its publication.) Work was hard to find. With no job and no money, Farzat survived on dwindling savings while living in a small room with a school friend from Hama. The room was barely large enough to hold a bed, so he and his friend slept in shifts. His friend worked during the day and slept at night, whereas Ali worked at night and slept during the day. This is the origin of Farzat's nocturnal work habits. Farzat's friends critiqued and admired his drawings. Eventually these caricatures began to win admission to exhibitions. And after six months of this regimen, Farzat landed a job at the Baath newspaper *Al-Thawra (The Revolution)*.

Since then, Ali Farzat's drawings have been featured in 28 exhibitions. For ten years beginning in 1990, his cartoons appeared six days per week on the editorial page of *Tishreen,* the largest Syrian newspaper. According to Syria-online.com, Farzat's "black humor" enjoys "extraordinary" appeal among Syrians. "By the late seventies, his caricatures became a daily ritual of Syrian cultural life: an angry, yet funny, outcry expressing all the frustrations and disappointments of the personal, national, and pan-Arab present-time problems."

Wisdom

By Bassem Taleb

I first met Ali Farzat in 1970 in Syria during our mandatory military service. We were assigned to work together on a conservative military magazine, *The People's Army.* Ali, the artist of the magazine, suggested to me, the editor, that he draw a caricature for the cover of the magazine. When I proposed the idea to our boss, however, he refused. "This is a serious publication," he said. At that point, I decided to quit.

Ali was born to draw. He has a gift, a presence, a magical touch. He is capable of drawing any time and any place—in the street, in a car, or at home.

One day in the early 1970s in Damascus, during our military service, we were listening to a lecture from a profusely-decorated high-ranking officer who talked about what it took to become a successful military leader. As you can guess, his performance was pro forma. We had heard all of this self-congratulatory talk before, and our minds were wandering. Some of those in the audience stifled yawns, others doodled on their note pads. Ali took a paper napkin and drew

The W🖤RLD

11 SEP.

تتصف المواضيع التي يرسمها علي ببعد النظر وعمق المحتوى وفاعلية التأثير . فعندما يرسم فتاة ريفية بسيطة على سبيل المثال فقد تتضمن خطوطه وتعابير الفتاة ما يشير إلى قضايا كبرى كالفساد أو الحرب أو البيئة ، أو العولمة أو التمييز العنصري .

ليس لرسوم علي عناوين وقلما يلجأ إلى الاتكال على الشروح والكلمات للوحة ته يفرض على المشاهد ويدعوه للتأمل والتفسير والمشاركة ، فقد يعني رسم واحد أموراً مختلفة للناس . كما تتميز رسوم علي بأنها لينة وانسيابية وقوية وذات تأثير عال في آن واحد معاً .

أفكار علي بسيطة وشاملة وتتناول الإنسان العادي رجلا كان أم امرأة ، طفلا كان أم كهلا ، ومع ذلك فهي عميقة ووجدانية وتستحوذ اهتمام المشاهدة العادي والناقد الفني ذي الثقافة العالية .

كذلك فإن مواضيعه تتصف بالعالمية ولا تحدها حدود قطرية أو إقليمية أو قارية لكنها بمجملها ذات إحساس مرهف لحال الفقراء والمحرومين وضد الاضطهاد والظلم في العالم .

حول العناوين والتعليقات
المحررون

يفضل علي فرزات أن يقدم صوره إلى العالم دون عناوين أو ملاحظات أو شروح أو تعليقات . وفي أعماله المنشورة في الجرائد يقوم فرزات بين الحين والآخر بخط ملاحظات بسيطة على شخص الكاريكاتير ولكنه نادرا ما يضيف شروحا . وشخوص فرزات ليست في العادة تصويرا مباشرا لشخصيات موجودة على أرض الواقع بل هي نقل لأنماط من الشخصيات لا الشخصيات ذاتها . في إبداعه ، يرسم فرزات صورا قابلة لتفسيرات متعددة . وخلو أعماله من عناوين يكسبها غموضا وقوة مما يضفي عليها سمة الفن .

وبعد ، فالكاريكاتير محاكاة ساخرة ، ولا يصل مضمونها إلى المشاهد إلا إذا كان على دراية نسبية بموضوع الفنان . ومن الصعب فهم رسوم تقوم على أحداث وقعت في الماضي كمجموعة الرسوم التي بين يدينا . ينطبق هذا القول خاصة على القراء الأمريكيين الذين قد يواجهون مشقة في فهم سياق بعض رسومها بعينها ، وهو سياق واضح المعالم لقراء فرزات من العرب الذين اعتادوا على مطالعة رسومه في الجرائد اليومية ليروا تعليقاته على أحداث الأسبوع ، تلك التعليقات اللاذعة والمتسمة بالطرافة في أغلب الأحوال .

وللمساهمة في إيضاح سياق الرسوم ، قمنا بتصنيف رسوم فرزات في فصول وأقسام . كما زودناها أحيانا بملاحظات تعكس الطريقة التي تفاعل بها القائمون على هذا العمل مع المضامين المطروحة . بعضنا عرب ، أحدنا عربي أمريكي ، واثنان منا أمريكيان خبرا الشرق الأوسط . وهذه العناوين والملاحظات هي من وضعنا نحن وليست لفرزات .

ومع ذلك هنالك استثناءان ، ففي عام 1989 اتهم صدام حسين علي فرزات بالسخرية منه والتهكم به فمنعه من دخول العراق والواضح أنه هدد حياته . ومنذ ذلك الحين دأب علي فرزات على تأييد سقوط صدام حسين ونشط في تصويره ووصف حكمه للعراق بعدد من الرسوم الساخرة .

16

two separate pictures, side by side, of the lecturer. In one of these, the lecturer was a highly confident man wearing a crisp uniform with medals, his chest puffed up as he spoke to an attentive audience. In the second picture the lecturer is at home in his underwear—no medals—his shoulders sagging, afraid and weak as he stands in front of his wife.

Ali's themes are far-reaching. When he draws a simple country girl, he could be referring to corruption, war, the environment, globalization, or discrimination. His drawings typically have no captions. This invites the viewer to participate. A single drawing will mean different things to different people. The lines of Ali's drawings, both supple and strong—touch the soul of the viewer.

Ali's ideas are simple and are comprehensible to the man or woman on the street. Yet his ideas are also profound and appeal to the highly-educated art critic. His themes are universal He is sensitive to the plight of the poor and disenfranchised. As a man, Ali is unpretentious and down to earth. He hates injustice, arrogance, and materialism. To Ali Farzat, art and life are sacred.

On Titles & Notes

By the editors.

Ali Farzat prefers to present his images to the world without labels, notes, captions, or commentary. In his commercially published work, Farzat occasionally scribbles notes on his figures but almost never provides captions. Farzat's figures are not normally identified with actual people—they depict types, not personalities. At his best, Farzat creates haunting images that give rise to multiple interpretations. Taken without labels, his work has the ambiguity and power that marks it as art.

Caricature, however, *is* parody. And parody does not succeed unless the viewer understands the object of the artist's attention. A retrospective collection such as the one in this book is difficult for readers (especially American readers) who may have a hard time grasping the context for individual drawings—a context that is clear to Farzat's Arab readers who open a newspaper on a given day to view Farzat's biting and often humorous commentary on the week's events.

As a practical help, we've grouped Farzat's drawings, given them chapter and section titles, and supplied occasional notes (and traditional sayings) that suggest some of the ways Farzat's drawings have affected those of us who have worked to pull this collection together. Several of us are Arabs, one is an Arab-American, and two are Americans with experience in the Middle East. These labels and notes are ours, not Farzat's.

There are two exceptions. In 1989 Ali Farzat was accused by Saddam Hussein of parodying him. Saddam barred Farzat from Iraq and threatened his life. Since then, Farzat has advocated Saddam's overthrow and has energetically depicted Saddam Hussein and his governance of Iraq in a number of unflattering caricatures. Following September 11th, Farzat produced a number of cartoons that referred to the terrorist attacks. Two have been included as illustrations in this introduction. Others are included in our chapter on 9-11.

إرهاب وطغاة

اعمل لدنياك كأنك تعيش أبدا و اعمل لآخرتك كأنك تموت غدا .

— قول عربي

I. Terror & Tyrants

"Work for this world as though you will live forever. And prepare for the hereafter as though you are dying tomorrow."
—Traditional Arabic saying

الدنيا مراية اوريها توريك .

—قول عربي

9-11
١١-٩

"The world is a mirror. Stand before it, and it will reflect your love, your hate, your tenderness, your rage."
—Traditional Arabic saying

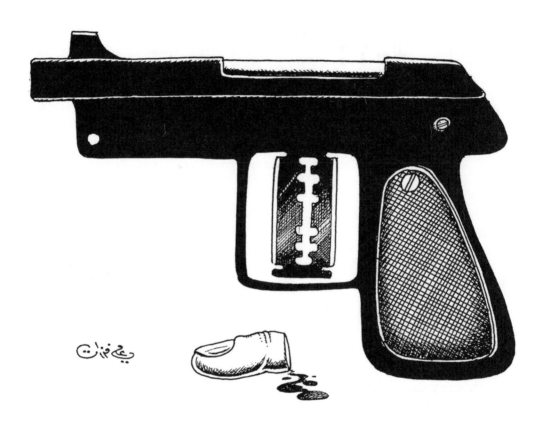

9-11

9-11

9-11

ما في طلعة إلا وراها نزلة .

— قول عربي

هذا المثل يمكن أن يشير إلى القائد الذين يستأثر بالحكم والجاه ،
ويعامل شعبه بوحشية ، ويسرق ثرواتهم ، ويحسب نفسه باق
إلى الأبد . لكنه يتجاهل حقيقة أنه "ما من طلعة إلا وراها نزلة" ،
يتجسد فيها فقدانه للنفوذ ، وانهيار السلطة ، كأنه يوم الحساب .

— صباح

Saddam 1990 - 2002

"Behind every hill there is a downhill."
—Traditional Arabic saying

In one use, this saying refers to a ruler who ascends in power and money, brutalizing his people, stealing their wealth, and thinking that he will ascend forever. He ignores the fact that behind every hill there is a downhill, a loss of influence, a decline in power, a day of reckoning.
—Sabah

7/17/1990

Saddam 1990 - 2002

12/9/1990

8/13/1995

Saddam 1990 - 2002

7/1/1996

SADDAM 1990 - 2002

33

12/10/1998

Saddam 1990 - 2002

9/12/1999

Saddam 1990 - 2002

35

3/25/2001

SADDAM 1990 - 2002

36

9/11/2002

Saddam 1990 - 2002

من قلة الخيل ركبوا عالكلاب سروج.

— قول عربي

Saddam 2003

"When horses are scarce, you saddle dogs!"
—Traditional Arabic saying

Notes

ملاحظات

3/24/2003

« الصورة »

Television Picture

« الأصل »

Reality

3/29/2003

Saddam 2003

4/12/2003

4/30/2003

SADDAM 2003

12/15/2003

SADDAM 2003

45

الدكتاتوريات

Dictatorships

12/20/2003

12/25/2003

SADDAM 2003

47

الجنة بلا ناس ما بتنداس.

—قول عربي

II. Life

"Paradise without people is worth nothing."
—Traditional Arabic saying

أنا الغريق فما خوفي من البلل .

—قول عربي

Human Nature

الطبيعة الإنسانية

"Since I am drowning, why should I fear getting wet?"
—Traditional Arabic saying

HUMAN NATURE

HUMAN NATURE

رب يوم بكيت منه فلما . . . صرت في غيره بكيت عليه .

— قول عربي

Modern Times

الأزمنة الحديثة

"There was a time when all I did was cry. Then things got worse. Now I cry for those good old times."
—Traditional Arabic saying

MODERN TIMES

MODERN TIMES

MODERN TIMES

وجه مليح ويأكل شي قبيح .

— قول عربي

" سقطت هويتك " .
يعني ان شخصيتك قد تغيرت .

— نجيب حلبي

Masks

"He has a fine face, but eats vile things."
—Traditional Arabic saying

When I was a young man in Aleppo, we used to kid our friends. "You've lost your ID card!" we would say—just like Americans would say, "You're crazy!" Of course, the person still had his card. What he had lost, in our joke, was his identity itself.
—Nagib Halabi

MASKS

MASKS

MASKS

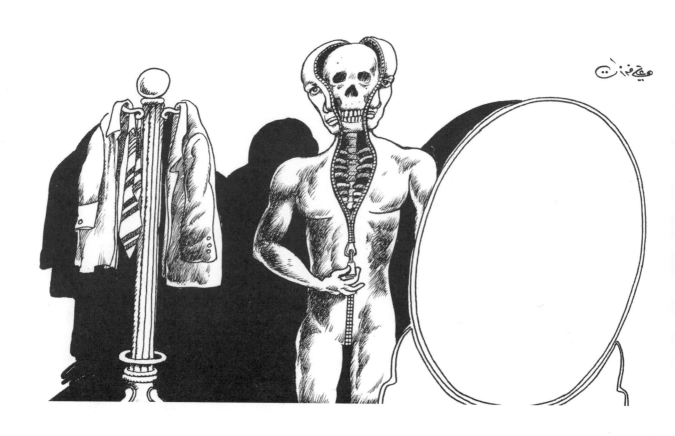

MASKS

MASKS

الحكومة

خير الناس من فرح للناس بالخير.

— قول عربي

III. Government

"He who rejoices in the welfare of others is the chosen of the people."
—Traditional Arabic saying

الامم الغبية تفعل برجالها كما يفعل الأطفال بلعبهم ، تحطمهم ثم تبكى طالبة غيرهم .

— انطون سعادة

كل يغني على ليله .

— قول عربي

فخار يكسر بعضه .

— قول عربي

هذان المثلان كثيرا ما يوجهان للقادة العرب وغيرهم من المسؤولين — الذين تعوزهم الوحدة والهارموني . فرجل الشارع ، بعد سماع أخبار آخر مؤتمر قمة عربي ، يجد نفسه راغبا أن يرفع يديه في الهواء قائلا : "ومن يبالي؟ ليقتتل الملوك والرؤساء العرب مع بعضهم البعض" .

— صباح

Presidents

"A stupid nation does to its leaders what children do to their toys. They break them, then cry for new ones."
    —Antoine Sa'ade

"Everyone is singing the way he likes."
    —Traditional Arabic saying

"Let the pottery smash itself."
    —Traditional Arabic saying

These two traditional sayings are often directed at Arab leaders and diplomats—who are frequently criticized for their lack of unity and harmony. After hearing news of the latest Arab summit, the common man is tempted to throw his arms in the air and say, "Who cares? Let the presidents fight among themselves."
    —Sabah

"Arab leaders, when driving their cars, signal to the left, then turn to the right."
—Often heard in Arab lands

Forty years ago, a wave of military coups brought Arab regimes to power. "The revolution," these leaders told us, "requires draconian changes—immediately."

What happened to this sense of urgency? Strangely enough, those who once championed sudden change have become defenders of the status quo. "We favor reform," they now tell us. "But reform must happen slowly—and we must be in charge."
—Nagib Halabi

إجعل الإشارة الى اليسار ولكن اذهب الى اليمين .
— اقوال شائعة في العالم العربي
أصحاب الثورات قالوا ان التغيير لابد منه في الحال ، وهكذا فعلوا والآن يطلب منهم التغيير فيستمهلون . . . فما الذي عدا مما بدى؟
— نجيب حلبي

PRESIDENTS

PRESIDENTS

PRESIDENTS

PRESIDENTS

PRESIDENTS

اذا كان الغراب دليل قوم . . . يمر بهم على جيف الكلاب .
— قول عربي

المال يتكلم والكرسي ايضا يتكلم .
— قول عربي

Ministers
of Government

"When crows guide the people, they lead them to the carcasses of dogs."
    —Traditional Arabic saying

"Money talks and the chair speaks."
    —Traditional Arabic saying

MINISTERS OF GOVERNMENT

MINISTERS OF GOVERNMENT

MINISTERS OF GOVERNMENT

97

ارقص للقرد في دولته.
— قول عربي
خزينة الدولة جيوب رعاياها .
— اقوال شائعة في العالم العربي

Bureaucrats

بيروقطيون

"When the monkey reigns, dance before him."
—Traditional Arabic saying

"The treasury of the government is in the pockets of the people."
—A common saying in Arab lands

BUREAUCRATS

BUREAUCRATS

BUREAUCRATS

BUREAUCRATS

BUREAUCRATS

اسقاه الخل بأجنحة الدبان.
— قول عربي

Public Servants

"The sun is hot, the rivers are dry, and the people thirst. What does the Ottoman government do to help? The Pasha gives us vinegar to drink upon the wings of flies."

—Traditional Arabic saying

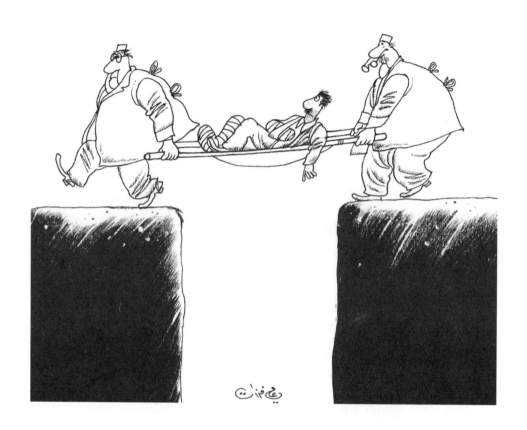

لا أمر لمن لا يطاع.
— قول عربي

Officers

"When you don't command obedience, don't issue orders."
—Traditional Arabic saying

OFFICERS

OFFICERS

121

OFFICERS

122

OFFICERS

123

المجتمع

كرامة لقصرك نهد خصنا .
— قول عربي

IV. Society

"For the sake of thy palace, shall we demolish our hut?"
—Traditional Arabic saying

كل واشرب وخلي الدنيا تخرب.

— قول عربي

The Rich

الأغنياء

"Eat and drink and let the world go to ruin."
—Traditional Arabic saying

THE RICH

THE RICH

THE RICH

THE RICH

THE RICH

THE RICH

تديله صباعك يطلب دراعك.
— قول عربي

Opportunists

المتسلقون

"Give him your finger, and he will demand your arm."
—Traditional Arabic saying

OPPORTUNISTS

Opportunists

OPPORTUNISTS

OPPORTUNISTS

OPPORTUNISTS

اعمل بحبة وحاسب البطال.

— قول عربي

Workers

"Work if only for a single grain and add to the profits of him who does nothing."
—Traditional Arabic saying

WORKERS

اللي يقول لمراته يا هانم يقابلوها على السلالم.

— قول عربي

Women

نساء

"If you treat your wife like a lady, all others will show her respect."
—Traditional Arabic saying

WOMEN

WOMEN

WOMEN

يهرب من الدب ، ليقع في الجب .

— قول عربي

وساقه من الحقل إلى البئر حيث ربطه إلى عجلة سحب الماء التي في أعلى البئر .
وقبل أن يتمكن الثور من سحب الماء خارت قوته ووقع على ركبه .

هرع رجل كان هناك إذ رأى ما جرى وقال لصاحب الثور إن الحر قد أهلك الثور فعليه
أن يرش رأسه بالماء حتى يصحو . فأجاب صاحب الثور قائلا : «نعم ، ولكن كيف
أرش الماء على رأسه وأنا لم أسحب الماء بعد . . . .»

— ول عربي

Simple Folk

بُسطاء

"He flees from the bear only to fall into the well."
— Traditional Arabic saying

One hot summer, a man needed water from the village well, so he took his ox from the field, led it to the well, and harnessed it to the water wheel atop the well. But before the ox could take a step to draw the water, it fell on its knees. A bystander rushed over.

"Your ox is exhausted from the heat," he said. "Sprinkle some water on its head immediately."

"Yes," said the man. "But before I can sprinkle water on its head, I must first draw the water from the well."

— Arabic proverb

SIMPLE FOLK

SIMPLE FOLK

SIMPLE FOLK

171

اللص العيار ما يسرق من حارته شي.

—قول عربي

V. World Problems

"The thief who understands his business does not steal from his quarter of the town."
—Traditional Arabic saying

أرى الناس يولون الغني كرامة

وإن لم يكن أهلا لرفعة مقدار

ويلوون عن وجه الفقير وجوههم

وإن كان أهلا أن يلاقى بإكبار

— من الشعر العربي

Hunger

I see people doing honor to the rich
Although they are not worthy of respect,
And averting their eyes from the face of the poor
Although they are worthy of admiration.

—Traditional Arabic saying

HUNGER

HUNGER

HUNGER

HUNGER

HUNGER

HUNGER

HUNGER

HUNGER

شجرة تستظل بها لا تدعي بقطعها .

— قول عربي

ما يزال صديقي الدمشقي يتذكر أرض جده في الغوطة (الواحة الخضراء التي وجدت
دمشق في كنفها) . كانت أرضا معطاء ، حسنة السقاية ، ومحاطة بالأشجار المثمرة .
لكن خلال السنوات الأربعين الأخيرة ، قطعت أشجارها ليحل محلها عمارات إسمنتية .
دمشق مثلها كمثل القاهرة وغيرها من المدن الرئيسة، توسعت على حساب الأرض
الطيبة . وتلوث ماؤها وهواؤها ، وغطى الإسمنت والإسفلت الأرض المعطاء .

— صباح

The Environment
البيئة

"A tree that affords thee shade, do not order it to be cut down."
—Traditional Arabic saying

A friend from Damascus still remembers his grandfather's land in al-Ghutah (the oasis where the city was founded). The land was rich, well-watered, and covered with fruit trees. In the last forty years, however, the orchards have been cut and row after row of concrete apartment buildings have been constructed. Damascus, like Cairo and other major cities, has spread to cover the land. The water is polluted, the air is polluted, and the land is covered with concrete and asphalt.
—Sabah

THE ENVIRONMENT

THE ENVIRONMENT

THE ENVIRONMENT

THE ENVIRONMENT

THE ENVIRONMENT

ابعد عن الشر وغني له .
— قول عربي

ذهب رجل ليزور صاحبه الذي يسكن قرب منزل مسؤول . قال
الصديق : "كن هناك في الموعد المحدد ولا تتأخر ، وإلا لن
تجدني انتظرك في الطريق ، وستكون أنت في مكان شبهة" .
لكن الرجل وصل متأخرا عشرة دقائق ، فوجد نفسه محاطا
بأربعة عناصر من المخابرات . انه لمن الحكمة أن يتحاشى المرء
هذا الضرب من الناس ، إلى أن يصل بيته آمنا .
—صباح

Civil Liberties

"Stay away from evil and sing to it."
    —Traditional Arabic saying

A man went to visit a friend who lived near the residence of a statesman. "Be right on time," the friend said. "Otherwise I will not be on the street to greet you, and you will come under suspicion." Sure enough, the man arrived ten minutes late and he was surrounded by four scowling secret policemen or *mukhabarat* and suffered some unpleasant moments before his friend came to rescue him.

It's always best to avoid such people. Then, after reaching the safety of home, you can sing softly to them.
    —Sabah

CIVIL LIBERTIES

CIVIL LIBERTIES

شرارة تحرق الحارة .

— قول عربي

قال أستاذ لطلابه : "لقد سقط العالم بيد الحمقى ، هؤلاء الذين يصنعون الأسلحة الفتاكة ، ويلعبون دور الله . لا شك أن عقول هؤلاء في خلفياتهم" .

ضحك الطلاب ، وسأل أحدهم : "وماذا يتعين علينا أن نفعل لنبقي عقولنا في رؤوسنا؟"

أجاب الأستاذ : "الأمر في منتهى السهولة . ليبق الله هو الله . ولنكبح أنفسنا عن الأفكار الشيطانية والأسلحة المهلكة . في هذه الحالة تبقى عقولنا في المكان الذي خلقها الله فيه" .

— صباح

Weapons

الأسلحة

"A single spark can burn the whole quarter."
—Traditional Arabic saying

A teacher said to his students, "The world has fallen into the hands of fools, those who invent deadly weapons and play God. No doubt their brains are in their asses."

His students laughed, and one of them said, "What should we do to keep our brains in our heads."

"It's easy," replied the teacher. "Let God be God. Refrain from devilish thought and deadly weapons. And your brains will stay where God put them."

—Sabah

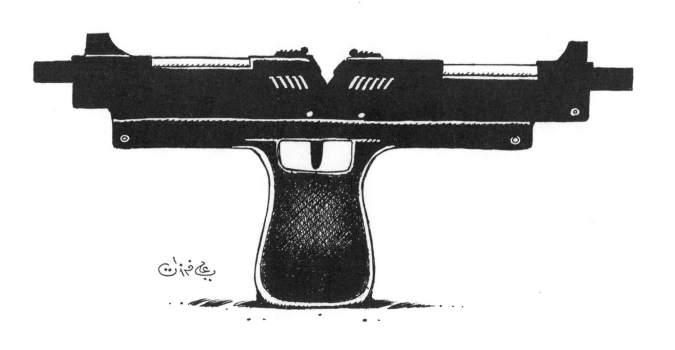

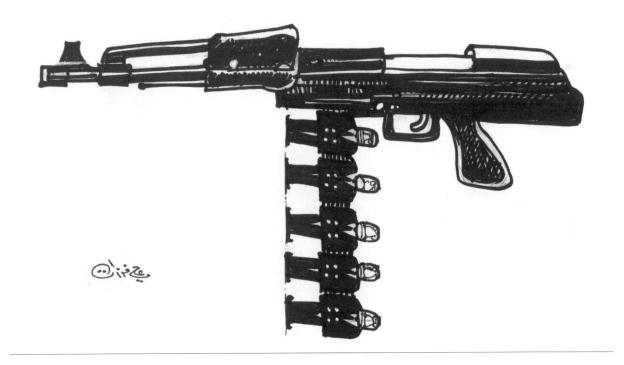

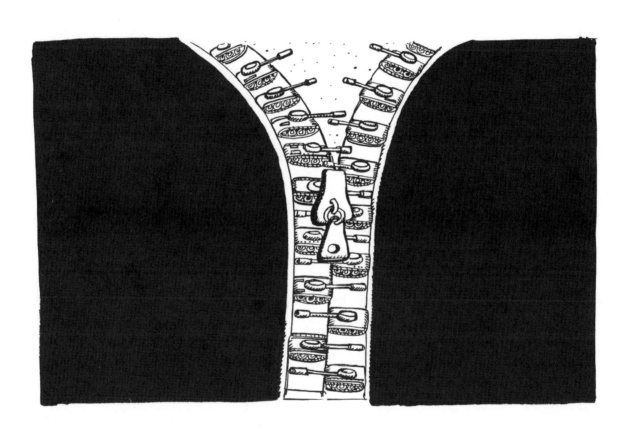

الخرق بالرفق يلحم .

— قول عربي

نمد جسومنا جسرا فقل للرفاق أن يعبروا .

— انطون سعادة

Peace

"With gentleness a quarrel is healed."
—Traditional Arabic saying

"We lay down our bodies as bridges for our comrades.
Tell them to pass safely."
—Antoine Sa'ade

PEACE

PEACE

PEACE

PEACE

PEACE

225

الحرب غشوم.

— قول عربي

رب وامعتصماه انطلقت ملء افواه الصبايا اليتم .

لامست اسماعهم لكنها لم تلامس نخوة المعتصم .

— عمر ابو ريشة

سلام من صبا بردى ارق .

ودمع لا يكفكف يا دمشق .

— احمد شوقي

War

"War is a demon."
> —Traditional Arabic saying

"A cry for help was coming from the mouths of orphaned boys and girls. This cry was heard by the rulers but it did not touch their hearts."
> —Omar Abu Risheh, chastizing Arab leaders and military officers for neglecting the victims of the 1948 war with Israel.

"I salute the River Barada. It is impossible for me to wipe the tears that are coming from the eyes of Damascus."
> —Ahmad Shawki, in 1920, after Syria's two-year-long independence was ended by French troops.

WAR

WAR

229

WAR

الملحق

Appendix

Acknowledgements

Brooke Anderson collected drawings from Ali Farzat in Damascus over two years' time and helped to shape the chapter divisions. George Meassy negotiated final edits and corrections with Ali Farzat and translated the introductions. Mamoun Sakkal of Sakkal Design provided the Thuluth style Arabic calligraphy. Sabah (the nom de plume of a writer originally from Damascus) helped find Arabic sayings and supplied several anecdotes. Nagib Halabi (the nom de plume of a businessman from Aleppo) provided traditional Arabic sayings as well as quotations from: Syrian/Lebanese political figure Antoine Sa'ade; Ahmad Shawki, the "Prince of Poets," from Cairo (d. 1932); and Omar Abu Risheh, the political poet and diplomat from Aleppo. We have relied on the work of Isa Khalil Sabbagh ("As the Arabs Say . . ." Volumes I and II) for many of the Arabic sayings on our title pages. Thanks to John Anderson, Lachlan Reed, Eric Soderlund, Holly Thomas and Richard Wood. Thanks as well to those we have missed.

Bibliography

Burckhardt, John Lewis. *Arabic Proverbs.* Mineola, NewYork: Dover, 2004. (AP)

Elkhadem, Saad. *Old Arabic Sayings, Similies, and Metaphors.* Fredericton, New Brunswick, Canada: York, 1991. (OASSM)

Sabbagh, Isa Khalil. *"As The Arabs Say . . ."* Volume I. Washington: Sabbagh Management Corp., 1983. (ATAS VI)

Sabbagh, Isa Khalil. *"As The Arabs Say . . ."* Volume II. Washington: Sabbagh Management Corp., 1985. (ATAS VII)

Citations & Notes

(Abbreviations key to the Bibliography and Acknowledgements. This list applies to unattributed sayings, proverbs, and anecdotes.)

Page #	Citation		
19	ATAS VI p11	127	AP #551 p 198
21	AP #49 p 16	137	ATAS VI p 55
29	Sabah	145	AP #55 p 18
39	ATAS VI p 33	153	ATAS VII p 36
49	ATAS VI p 27	163	AP #723 p 256]
51	ATAS VII p 18	173	AP #28 p 9
59	ATAS VII p24	175	Sabah
69	AP715, p 253	185	AP #361 p 113
77	AP #246 p 78	197	Sabah
79	Sabah	211	Sabah
80	Halabi	219	AP #247 p 78
91	AP #525 p 190	229	OASSM 52
91	Halabi		
99	AP #87 p 28		
99	Halabi		
109	AP #85 p 27		
117	ATAS VI p 58		
125	AP #553, p 199		

Ali Farzat

1951   Born in the city of Hama, 200 km north of Damascus.

1963   First professional drawing appeared on the front page of *Al-Ayyam (The Days)*.

1969   Began drawing caricatures for *Al-Thawra (The Revolution)*.

1970   Began studies in drawing in the Faculty of Fine Arts at Damascus University.

1973   Left Damascus University during his third year.

1973   Married Ayda Ansari of Damascus (two sons and two daughters).

1980   Became Director of *Rabitat Arrassameen Alkarirater Al-Arab* (the Society of Arab Cartoonists).

1980   First prize. Intergraphic International Festival, Berlin, Germany.

1980   His caricatures begin to appear in *Le Monde,* as well as other international publications.

1980   First prize at the first Caricature Festival of Damascus.

1982   First prize at the second Caricature festival of Damascus.

1984   Animated an anti-air pollution and anti-litter commercial for Qatari TV.

1985   Exhibit, Syrian Cultural Center, Moscow.

1985   Third prize at the Capravo International Festival, Bulgaria.

1987   First prize for a caricature at the Sofia International Festival, Bulgaria.

1989   Exhibit L'Institut du Monde Arabe, Paris, France. (Received a death threat in connection with this exhibit. Banned from Iraq, Jordan, and Libya because of one cartoon in this exhibit.)

1990   Began work for *Tishreen*, one of Syria's state-owned daily newspapers.

1990   Gold medal for the Best Arab caricaturist, awarded by the Middle Eastern Press Establishment.

1991   Gold medal for the Best Arab Caricaturist, awarded by the Middle Eastern Press Establishment.

1991   His drawings appeared frequently in Gulf Arab papers.

1994   Selected as one of the five best caricaturists in the world at an international arts festival in Morg, Switzerland.

2001   Began publishing *Ad-Domari (The Lamplighter)*, a satirical newspaper that was heralded as the first independent publication in Syria since 1963.

2003   Presented with the 2002 Prince Claus Award.

2003   *Ad-Domari* ceases publication after its license is revoked by the Syrian government.

سيرة علي فرزات

1951	: ولد في مدينة حماة التي تبعد 200 كيلومترا إلى الشمال من دمشق .
1963	: في أوائل الستينات ظهر له أول رسم كمحترف على الصفحة الأولى لجريدة "الأيام" .
1969	: بدأ يرسم الكاريكاتير لجريدة الثورة .
1970	: بدأ دراسته للرسم في كلية الفنون الجميلة بجامعة دمشق .
1973	: ترك جامعة دمشق في العام الثالث من دراسته .
1973	: تزوج بعائدة الأنصاري من دمشق . وقد أنجبا صبيين وبنتين .
1980	: صار رئيساً لرابطة الرسامين الكاريكاتير العرب .
1980	: نال الجائزة الأولى في المهرجان العالمي . . . برلين ، ألمانيا .
1980	: بدأت رسومه الكاريكاتورية تظهر في جريدة اللوموند إضافة إلى جرائد عالمية أخرى .
1980	: نال الجائزة الأولى في المهرجان الأول للكاريكاتير بدمشق .
1982	: نال الجائزة الأولى في المهرجان الثاني للكاريكاتير بدمشق .
1984	: أحيا مقاومة تلوث الهواء و الفضلات التجارية للتلفزيون القطري .
1985	: أقام معرضا في مركز الثقافة السورية في موسكو .
1985	: نال الجائزة الثالثة في مهرجان كبرافو الدولي في بلغاريا .
1987	: نال الجائزة الأولى في مهرجان صوفيا الدولي في بلغاريا .
1989	: أقام معرضا في معهد العالم العربي ، باريس ، فرنسا . (وتلقى تهديدا بالقتل من جراء هذا المعرض وحظر من دخول العراق والأردن وليبيا بسبب إحدى الصور الكاريكاتيرية في هذا المعرض .)
1990	: بدأ العمل في جريدة تشرين وهي إحدى الصحف التي تملكها الدولة .
1990	: نال الميدالية الذهبية لأفضل رسام كاريكاتير عربي من مؤسسة الشرق الأوسط للطباعة .
1991	: نال أيضاً الميدالية الذهبية لأفضل رسام كاريكاتير عربي من مؤسسة الشرق الأوسط للطباعة .
1991	: ظهرت رسوماته في الصحف الخليجية العربية .
1994	: انتخب كأحد أفضل الرسامين الكاريكاتيريين الخمسة في العالم وذلك في مهرجان مورج في سويسرا .
2001	: شرع بنشر جريدة الدومري وهي أول جريدة سورية مستقلة منذ عام 1963 .
2003	: استلم جائزة الأمير كلاوس التي نالها عام 2002 .
2003	: توقفت جريدة الدومري عن الصدور بعد أن ألغت الحكومة السورية رخصتها .

Index

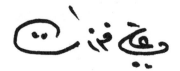

Ali Farzat is one of the leading political cartoonists of the Arab world. His work has appeared for thirty-five years in major Arab daily newspapers as well as in *Le Monde* and other international publications. Farzat has served as the head of the Society of Arab Cartoonists since 1980 and has won many awards, including the prestigious Prince Claus Award in 2002. Farzat is Shakespearean in his productivity. He has created more than 15,000 caricatures. He is now in his fifties and lives in Damascus with his wife and family.

علي فرزات أحد رواد الكاريكاتير السياسي في العالم العربي . ولقد ظهرت أعماله على مدى أربعين عاما في الجرائد العربية اليومية واللوموند وغيرها من وسائل الإعلام المطبوعة العالمية . يشغل فرزات منصب رئيس اتحاد الكاريكاتيريين العرب منذ عام 1980 ، وقد نال جوائز عديدة منها جائزة الأمير كلاوس الرفيعة . هذا ، وفرزات شكسبيري في غزارة انتاجه ، فقد وضع أكثر من 15000 رسما كاريكاتوريا . وهو الآن في العقد الخامس من العمر ويعيش مع زوجته في دمشق .